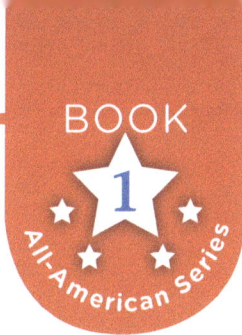

BOOK 1

All-American Series

I0189946

Symbols of Freedom

By Gene & Bobbie Carnell

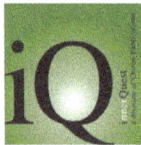

© 2017 by innerQuest, an imprint of Chiron Publications. All rights reserved. No part of this publication may be reproduced, stored in a retrieval system, or transmitted, in any form by any means, electronic, mechanical, photocopying, recording, or otherwise, without the prior written permission of the publisher, Chiron Publications, 932 Hendersonville Road, Suite 104, Asheville, North Carolina 28803.

innerQuestBooks.com
ChironPublicatons.com

innerQuest is a book imprint of Chiron Publications
Edited by Jennifer Fitzgerald
Interior and cover design by Lisa Alford
Printed primarily in the United States of America.

If you are an organization wishing to buy bulk quantities of this book, please contact Chiron Publications at generalmanager@chironpublications.com

ISBN 978-1-63051-432-7 paperback

Library of Congress Cataloging-in-Publication Data Pending

Some art courtesy of Freepik.com and the New York Public Library Digital Collection

Dedicated to all our
young "nieces" and "nephews"
across this land.

All-American Series

The Symbols of Freedom

America is all about family: living, playing, working and worshiping together in harmony and cooperation. Our national motto affirms this–E PLURIBUS UNUM–"Out of Many, One!"

UNITED WE STAND, DIVIDED WE FALL. In other words, good will and love bring peace. Selfishness and anger cause us all pain.

Besides our immediate family—parents, sisters and brothers—we have relatives who live in other places. This includes grandparents, uncles, aunts, even cousins. How big is your family?

Boys and girls, meet your—and everybody's—favorite Uncle, Uncle Sam.

He's a popular folk hero and a sort of national treasure. He came to stand for all the good things about America: loyalty, honesty, fairness, respect, love of country and patriotism.

These are qualities of life that make us better as a people.

SAMUEL WILSON, a meatpacker from Troy, New York, supplied barrels of beef to the Army during the War of 1812.

He stamped each of his barrels with U.S., and "UNCLE SAM" was born. He became the inspiration for the model and ideal of America's "Patriotic-Patriarch."

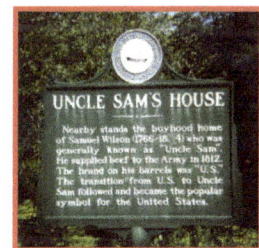

UNCLE SAM'S HOUSE

Nearby stands the boyhood home of Samuel Wilson (1766-18..4) who was generally known as "Uncle Sam". He supplied beef to the Army in 1812. The brand on his barrels was U.S. The transition from U.S. to Uncle Sam followed and became the popular symbol for the United States.

A PATRIOT IS SOMEONE WHO LOVES HIS OR HER COUNTRY ENOUGH TO DEFEND IT!

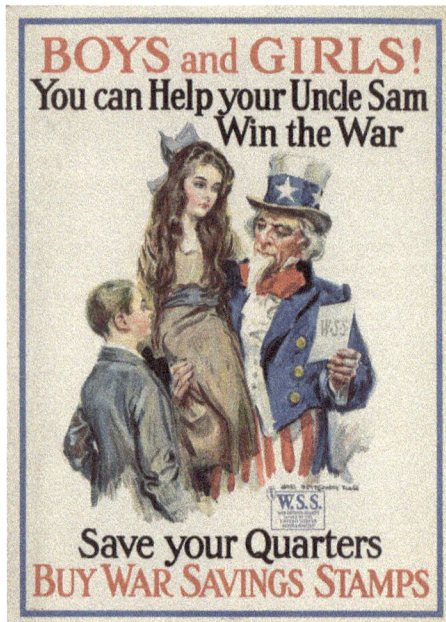

BOYS and GIRLS!
You can Help your Uncle Sam
Win the War

W.S.S.

Save your Quarters
BUY WAR SAVINGS STAMPS

Artists, like Thomas Nast, drew Uncle Sam with a long beard, big top hat, blue coat, and red-white-and-blue striped pants. He became a Yankee Doodle-like character and an enduring symbol. Just what is a symbol?

A symbol is a word, picture or object that stands for something very special. It is a visual reminder or illustration like the icons on your computer screen. You probably could recognize many "logos" before words. Can you think of any?

THE STATUE OF LIBERTY is a physical symbol of our nation and its commitment to "liberty and justice for all." The "Lady" is hostess to nearly 4 million visitors a year.

UNCLE SAM is a flesh and blood ideal of national unity and strength. He represents 321 million members of the American family.

When we speak of the U.S. we think of Uncle Sam. In fact all government property, from airplanes to ammunition, carpets to computers, and vehicles to uniforms, are referred to as belonging to "Uncle Sam."

And Uncle Sam has a wife. Her name is Aunt Samantha, his partner and helper—a very important job. Women are patriots too!

Long before the Revolution, men and women were forming individual ideas about freedom. Most often the Founding Fathers led the way publicly while the Supporting Mothers exercised influence privately. Each played an important role in helping us gain our liberty and in maintaining it.

AUNT SAMANTHA AND UNCLE SAM WORK TOGETHER. Teamwork is always better in every area of life.

Now our Armed Forces have both men and women on the front lines sharing the duties and responsibilities of protecting our country.

Probably the most beautiful symbol of freedom is our flag.

The Red, White and Blue
Stands for all that's true;
It flies high in the breeze
And towers above the trees.
It fills us with pride,
And makes us feel good inside

OUR FLAG HAS BEEN KNOW AS "OLD GLORY" SINCE 1824, SO-CALLED BY SEA CAPTAIN WILLIAM DRIVER OF MASSACHUSETTS.

"...THAT OUR FLAG WAS STILL THERE..."

The flag that flew over Fort McHenry near the Baltimore, Maryland, harbor was indeed unusual. It had 15 stars and 15 stripes on it, not the 13 striped version we now have. Why? They added stars and stripes when new states came into the Union. But after Vermont (14) and Kentucky (15), they said "it's going to get too large," and they went back to the original design and added only stars.

This flag was the inspiration for our national anthem, written by Francis Scott Key in 1814.

STUDENTS LIKE YOU VOTED 2 TO 1 TO MAKE THE STAR SPANGLED BANNER OUR NATIONAL ANTHEM IN 1931.

I hope you fly our flag at your house every day, and not just on special occasions.

If you do, be sure to light it at night out of respect. It's required in our Flag Code, the rules and regulations governing the display of the flag.

Our flag had 48 stars on it for many years, six rows of eight stars, with points of each star pointing up. This was by executive order of President Taft in 1912.

FIVE POINT STARS WERE THE IDEA OF A WELL-KNOWN UPHOLSTERER IN HER DAY, ELIZABETH GRISCOM ROSS ASHBURN CLAYPOOLE, KNOWN TO US AS "BETSY ROSS."

Actually, the STARS AND STRIPES were raised for the very first time in America at Fort Stanwix, New York, on August 2, 1777. That would make a great trivia question wouldn't it? See if your parents knew this.

The current 50-star flag was designed in 1958 by a high school student named ROBERT G. HEFT for a school project.

His teacher gave him only a "B", perhaps for "Beautiful," huh? I would have given him an "A" for "American!"

You're A Grand Old Flag

George M. Cohan, the great musical flag-waver, draped himself in an American flag as he danced and sang a song in its honor. He got the idea in 1906 from a Civil War veteran who had been a Union color-bearer (flag holder). It is a lively march and good 'ole American "feel-good" music, now nearly a century old.

> You're a grand old flag
> You're a high-flying flag,
> And forever in peace may you wave.
> You're the emblem of the land I love,
> The home of the free and the brave.
> Every heart beats true
> 'Neath the Red, White and Blue,
> Where there's never a boast or a brag
> But should auld acquaintance be forgot,
> Keep your eye on the grand old flag.

★ ★   ★ ★   ★ ★   ★ ★   ★ ★   ★ ★   ★ ★   ★ ★   ★ ★   ★ ★   ★ ★

> This is the land where hate should die –
> No feuds of faith, no spleen of race,
> No darkly brooding fear should try
> Beneath our flag to find a place.

—Denis A. McCarthy

The Uncle Sam we see today is an artist's version of an earlier political cartoon done, believe it or not, by James Montgomery Flagg, with two g's. He sold his first illustration when he was only 12 years old. Can you imagine? It's true!

When World War I broke out, he was too old to fight. He made a contribution in another way. He provided patriotic posters in support of the war effort. He drew his first "I Want You" poster in 1917.

Have you seen one of them?

BUY WAR BONDS

Here's another famous poster done in 1942 by a man named N.C. Wyeth. He drew pictures for several books like Treasure Island, Robin Hood, The Deerslayer, and Robinson Crusoe.

Have you read any of these yet? They're great and when you get older, I hope you will. I know you'll enjoy them.

Remember, pictures are great symbols of ideas and ideals. Ideas are thoughts; Ideals are perfect absolute thoughts that have been proven good and true over time. Here are some examples:

Idea – wanting freedom
Ideal – having freedom

Idea – is a thought
Ideal – is a suitable action

See the difference?

Unfortunately, when some people—or nations—hungry for world power, take from their neighbors or try to rule them by force or fear, wars often result. America had to defend its way of life on many occasions from such enemies.

And wars are very expensive to wage. Everyone has to chip in and help out. During World War I citizens raised $17 billion dollars in LIBERTY BONDS. In the second World War, Americans bought $49 billion worth.

A BOND is simply a promise or a contract. Americans loaned the government the money it needed and they paid it back later with interest. Liberty bonds gave way to war bonds to help finance the war effort.

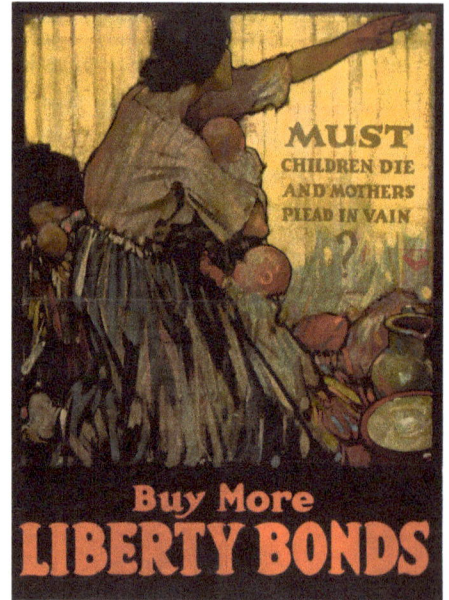

MUST CHILDREN DIE AND MOTHERS PLEAD IN VAIN

Buy More
LIBERTY BONDS

> "PEACE IS NOT JUST THE ABSENCE OF WAR. PEACE OCCURS WHEN EVIL IS CONTAINED, WHATEVER THE COST. FREEDOM ISN'T FREE!"

There were a lot of bond drives to encourage people to get involved, eight in fact.

Buy A Bond! Buy American!

Every school child could have a part in helping out. You could buy a defense stamp for 10 cents and put it in a booklet.

When you got $18.70 worth, you could add a nickel to it and turn it in for a $25 defense (war) bond. This was mine in the third grade and it still has $3.30 worth of stamps in it.

Now war bonds are called SAVINGS BONDS. They are a great way to save and help America at the same time.

Oftentimes good things come out of bad ones, don't they? Ask Mom what it means to "save for a rainy day." Aunt Samantha and I hope you learn the lessons of thrift and responsibility in the use of your money. All of us won't have the same amount, so we'll need to manage what we have and spend wisely. A debt is easy to get into, but hard to get out of. We must all live within our means – "on a budget."

THE GREEK WORD FOR EAGLE IS AETOS, "TO BLOW AS THE WIND OR BECOME ONE WITH THE WIND." TRULY, HE IS THE "MONARCH OF THE AIR" AND THE KING OF BIRDS.

Another visual image that helps us feel patriotic is the great majestic eagle.

He is strong and graceful and his lofty picture appears everywhere—even on our old quarters.

His wing span can reach 8 feet! With his proud head and sharp eyesight he reminds us of how important our vision ought to be. When you talk to someone, look them in the eye!

Male and female eagles "marry" for life and he makes a great father, too. The feathers on the head and upper part of the neck are white, thus the name "BALD" EAGLE.

He is our bird of freedom!

There are many important symbols of freedom. THE WASHINGTON MONUMENT, at just over 555 feet in height, is a very familiar landmark. It is the second tallest masonry (stone) structure in the world. And it is the most prominent feature of our nation's capital landscape.

The cornerstone was laid in 1848 with the same trowel George Washington himself used to lay the cornerstone of the Capitol building. It took nearly 40 years to complete because of the costs.

I climbed to the top when I visited Washington D.C. many years ago as a teenager. There are 898 steps. I counted them! I hope you can go there with you class or parents one day. It is a very unique experience.

Still another powerful icon of liberty is "THE BELL." The Liberty Bell, weighing over 2,000 pounds and made of ancient bronze, was cast (made) in London but arrived in America already cracked. It had to be redone locally and now hangs in a pavilion in Philadelphia's Independence National Historic Park.

It was hung there in 1976 for our nation's 200th birthday, called the bi-centennial. It rang to announce important events and in celebration. It is the most famous bell in the whole world.

It pealed out our independence when we decided to run our own affairs without outside interference.

It is over 3 feet high and was rang jubilantly following our Declaration over 227 years ago.

6078. OLD LIBERTY BELL.

Samantha and I hope you will continue to read more, study hard and find out all you can about our country. It truly is "the land of the free and the home of the brave," and it is OURS!

In our next book, we'll tell you about all the opportunities you will have for a career, and the many things you can do as an adult right here in America.

We love you and want you to always be patriotic!

Remember, we are the United States of America—symbolically and actually. By sharing common interests and goals, by respecting one another and by being good citizens ourselves, we really are ONE.

Oliver Wendell Holmes, beloved American poet, wrote:

> "ONE FLAG, ONE LAND,
> ONE HEART, ONE HAND,
> ONE NATION EVERMORE."

America is a great place in which to live and learn. There is excitement and beauty everywhere you go. It is a wonderful country! Here's some more dramatic history from A to Z; An All-American Alphabet Adventure.

A IS FOR THE ALAMO, where freedom took a stand; the cost was high as always...to the very last man.

B IS FOR BUNKER HILL, where The Revolution began, once committed to "never retreat," that was their plan.

C IS FOR OUR NATION'S CAPITOL, shining stately in the night, it is a symbol of a people standing for the right.

D IS FOR THE DISTRICT OF COLUMBIA, which is the people's home, here the law's applied to all and not just to some.

E IS FOR THE EAGLE, America's keen-eyed stately bird, he stands and watches proudly when love for America is heard.

F IS FOR THE FREEDOM TRAIL winding thru old Boston-town, where many early patriots agreed to never let her down.

G IS FOR OUR GOVERNMENT...of, by, and for us all, and makes us easier to see when we all stand up...and tall!

H IS FOR OUR HOMES, where we are loved and secure, we must all work together to see that they endure.

I IS FOR THE ISLAND where our Statue of Liberty stands, welcoming with open arms the oppressed from other lands.

J IS FOR JUSTICE, whose halls are The Supreme Court, they decide what is right and then give their report.

K IS FOR KITTY HAWK, where two brothers actually dreamed, and really flew an "airplane"… forever it seemed.

L IS FOR LINCOLN, our President; the sixteenth, he preserved the Union because of his great strength.

M IS FOR THE METHODISTS, whose roots run deep in Georgia state, their message was simple: "Love's stronger than hate!"

N IS FOR NEW YORK, where 8 million live and work in peace, its safety was shattered, but its patriotism never ceased.

O is for Ohio, birthplace of seven of our presidents, they call the "Buckeye State" home because they were residents.

P IS FOR PHILADELPHIA, the place where Freedom's bell was rung, and folks swell up with pride when a patriotic song is sung.

Q IS FOR QUANTICO, where a few proud men and women train and wait; because whenever freedom's threatened, they don't want to be late!

R IS FOR RUSHMORE, where heroes of the past gaze across the plain, reminding all who come to view, it was worth the pain.

S IS FOR OUR SYNAGOGUES, where Jewish friends go to pray, because freedom to practice religion is the American way.

T IS FOR TRUTH, on which all of our future rests, it is the only standard that will help us pass the test.

U IS FOR UNCLE SAM, symbol of national pride and unity, he embodies all that is good and right about this country.

V IS FOR VICTORY, and each one had its price, like pieces in a puzzle, it makes the picture nice.

W IS FOR WASHINGTON, first in the hearts of men, when he went off to war, he determined only to win.

X IS FOR X-RAY and can even look inside your heart, and God above is watching us to see if we will do our part.

Z IS FOR ZEST that adds joy to all of life, and makes marriages happier between husband and wife.

And now you've traveled across this land, and seen many places from A to Z, But the best part about our joyful journey was to remind us of just how great we still can be.

Just for fun, see if you can find these places mentioned on a big map of the United States. (there are two for DC and two for the Boston area).

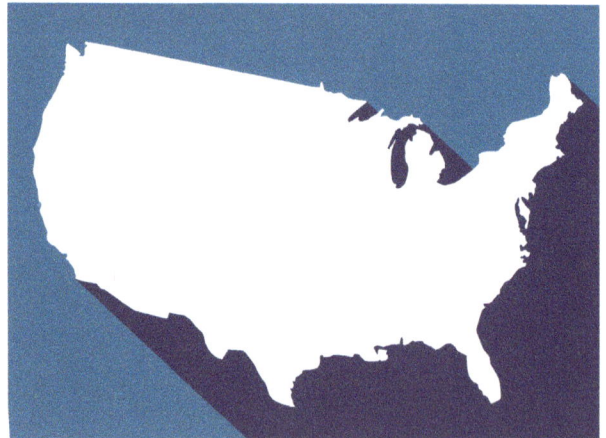

LESSONS FOR LIFE

1. Success requires discipline and good conduct.
2. Rules are made for order and peace.
3. Freedom is a personal privilege with public duties.
4. Visual reminders help our understanding.
5. "Uncle" is a term of friendship and respect—one who is older and wiser.

www.ingramcontent.com/pod-product-compliance
Lightning Source LLC
Chambersburg PA
CBHW051310020426
42331CB00018B/3490